UNDERSTANDING

YOUR
11 YEAR-OLD

YOUR
11 YEAR-OLD

Eileen Orford

Warwick Publishing
Toronto   Los Angeles

ISBN 1-894020-11-1

Published by:
Warwick Publishing Inc., 388 King Street East, Toronto, Ontario M5V 1K2
Warwick Publishing Inc., 1424 N. Highland Avenue, Los Angeles, CA 90027

Distributed by:
Firefly Books Ltd., 3680 Victoria Park Avenue, Willowdale, Ontario M2H 3K1

First published in Great Britain in 1993 by:
Rosendale Press Ltd.
Premier House
10 Greycoat Place
London SW1P 1SB

Design: Diane Farenick

Printed and bound in Canada

CONTENTS

Tavistock Clinic

The Tavistock Clinic, London, was founded in 1920, in order to meet the needs of people whose lives had been disrupted by the First World War. Today, it is still committed to understanding people's needs though, of course, times and people have changed. Now, as well as working with adults and adolescents, the Tavistock Clinic has a large department for children and families. This offers help to parents who are finding the challenging task of bringing up their children daunting and has, therefore, a wide experience of children of all ages. It is firmly committed to early intervention in the inevitable problems that arise as children grow up, and to the view that if difficulties are caught early enough, parents are the best people to help their children with them.

Professional Staff of the Clinic were, therefore, pleased to be able to contribute to this series of books to describe the ordinary development of children, to help in spotting the growing pains and to provide ways that parents might think about their children's growth.

INTRODUCTION

Eleven may seem to many a rather uninteresting age, when children are neither the appealing small creatures they used to be, nor the interesting, independent adolescents they will be. The twelfth year of life is nevertheless a time of change, when children are preparing for the adolescent upheavals to come.

Eleven year-olds have a number of adjustments to make during this year, and how they are able to manage them is crucial to how they will weather the adolescent years ahead.

CHAPTER ONE

WHAT ARE ELEVEN YEAR-OLDS LIKE?

On Tim's eleventh birthday, he felt a little confused. When he was ten, he had been very excited about reaching double figures. Now he was eleven. He had heard all about teenagers, but he wasn't one of them. Where was he? This is sometimes a problem for both parents and children alike.

Eleven is an in-between age for all children. Childhood is beginning to be over. But adolescence has not quite begun for most eleven year-olds. It is true that menstruation sometimes starts as young as nine years, but this is the exception. By eleven some girls, but not most, will be into puberty, and very few boys will be anywhere near adolescent at this age.

Differences in response to change

What is it that makes for such variation at this age? Physical development is, of course, one very important aspect. But there are many others. Some factors are quite external to the nature and feeling of the child concerned, such as parental attitude to this stage of development. Yet others may be hidden within the child's emotional development. The factors that determine the uniqueness of each one of us are buried in the history of our lives and in our responses to what has happened to us. Some we are aware of and can try to control. Some we are not aware of and are all the more powerful for operating without our conscious knowledge. Our feelings and experiences, derived in this complex way, make us what we are as individuals and drive us in the directions our lives take.

At eleven, children's individual patterns of response are well established and make them who they are. What is different at eleven is that children are beginning to discover and recognize this. Not only are they able to think about themselves and begin to appreciate their own individuality and particular capacities, but they are also able to appreciate those of others. This change in their way of thinking about themselves comes into being at about the same time as the huge spurt in physical development around the onset of adolescence, and frequently together with changes in the character of their education. It is not surprising that one eleven year-old may not seem much like another. Even the same responses to change may spring from many different inner situations.

Mary, for example, was young for her age, and seemed a bit reluctant to be as independent and mature as her contemporaries. Mary was the eldest of a large family and had always taken a lot of responsibility for her younger brothers and sisters. She had a good friend Rani with whom she shared some of her worries. Yet Rani's position was different. She was the youngest of a large family of brothers and sisters. Rani had always been the darling of her brothers and sisters, indulged and looked after by all. Her position as baby of the family was guarded by them. No wonder *she* did not want to grow up.

Fortunately the mothers of these two girls were friends who often talked together about their daughters. Rani's mom secretly felt a little shocked by the amount of responsibility that fell onto Mary's shoulders, while Mary's mother was rather critical of what she thought was Rani's mother's failure to foster her daughter's independence. They were both concerned by the girls' anxieties about moving into sixth grade. Discussing this, they drew each other's attention to how, on the one hand, Mary needed a bit of help to be a child because of the danger she was in of missing some of her carefree years. On the other hand, Rani was in danger of being so much the baby of the family that her growing up might be held back. Both parents made an effort to alter their approach so that Mary could begin to enjoy not having to take too much responsibility, while Rani was encouraged to see her move there as a step on the way to growing up.

Families and the eleven year-old

Children at this age are beginning to feel the need to get themselves together and to move away from being as dependent on their families as they had been. They need to find out who they are and to establish themselves in their own right and to start thinking about what *they* want for themselves and are good at. They also need to face what they are not so good at and what needs to be worked on. Is what interests *them* the same as the shared family concerns or is it something that is special for them? This may cause some friction from time to time.

Stewart, for example, had for a long time shared his family's interest in bird-watching. The whole family, including his younger sister, was used to spending time together on weekends and, during vacations in the wilderness with their binoculars. Stewart had become increasingly disinclined to join the family outings. He always seemed to have other things going on. His parents could understand and manage this on weekends, but it became a real problem at vacation time. The family was not very pleased when he insisted on taking his noisy Walkman on all their nature walks. For Stewart, his music kept him in touch with the friends and different activities that were now very important to him.

It is not just interests that eleven year-olds start developing for themselves; many at this age begin to have ideas about what is right behavior that are different from those of their parents. These differences may be awkward, but they can also be an important means by which eleven year-olds can sort out their own ideas. If this is to happen the eleven year-old must be able to talk with parents in a reasonably open and friendly way. Parents who are shocked or too heavily disapproving of the wilder ideas of their eleven year-old may not help the youngster to reach a balanced view of things. At eleven, many youngsters are just beginning to be able to put their more complex ideas into words, making it possible to differ from their parents, to sustain discussion and so develop these ideas.

Stewart, who was fed up with his parents' bird-watching holidays, was able to say so though not always in a very tactful way! He talked of his interest in birds, but also of his feeling that this was old-fashioned and he became scornful of his sister and his parents and their enthusiasm. His parents felt a bit hurt by what he said but were able to acknowledge his changing interests and to help him still to find something of value about what now seemed a thing of the past. As an eleven year-old, Stewart could not be left behind during the holidays, but discussions between him and his parents enabled them to find some compromise. Otherwise, a rebellious Stewart might not have had a good family vacation at all, and the rest of the family might have felt that theirs was spoiled by Stewart's discontent.

It is important for families to sort out issues like this, because eleven year-olds do need parents, however much they may feel that they can manage on their own. Parents may be tempted to go along with their children's conviction that they are big now and can organize things for themselves, but they (both parents and children) will soon find that this is not so. While children at this age should be able to cope with much of their physical care, they still need their parents' support and to know that parents are there to turn to in trouble. They need their parents to help them explore and understand their developing skills and relationships. They need them to talk to as Stewart did with his mom and dad. They need their parents as an accepting base from which to move outwards and to know that they are concerned, even though at the same time they may be wanting to assert their independence.

At this age, as they begin to move away emotionally and to invest more and more in groups of children of their own age, children paradoxically often become more aware of their families. Eleven year-olds may be very conscious of their families' peculiarities (as they judge them). Detailed instructions may be given about how parents are to behave with their friends or at school functions. Mother, perhaps, is expected to look young and be intelligent—or perhaps she is expected *not* to look too young and to impress school teachers. Whatever it is, it is all part of the effort of her son or daughter to define him or herself, apart from her.

As part of their general development and moves to confront growing up, eleven year-olds who are adopted or who are for some reason not with their birth parents may become increasingly interested in knowing about them. At this age they will not be able to have social work help to trace their birth parents, but questions to adoptive parents may become more insistent. It may be helpful for the adoptive parents to see, and even welcome, such moves at this age as part of their children's attempt to get themselves together and to assess their life rather than a wish to move away from them.

Families of all eleven year-olds may notice a change in their child's attitude to them, and may need to tolerate their clumsy first moves to leave the nest.

Gender development

Crucial to the development of children's feelings of identity is their understanding of themselves as a boy or as a girl. Ideas of what it is to be a woman or a man are particularly critical when children are eleven. More or less throughout their primary schooling children have got together in groups of the same sex. Boys and girls keep separate at this stage of their lives. Such groups establish their own standards of behavior considered acceptable for boys and for girls. These standards are fundamentally based on what each child brings from home, for the model of how men and women should behave derives from children's observations of and researches into their parents' behavior over the years. In the case of single parents, their ideas of the other sex will be crucial to the concept of the missing parent that the children will have. Experience of grandparents, uncles and aunts, teachers and others will also be important, but if the single parent is able to maintain a notion in the family of a good missing partner, then this will reinforce the image the children have of members of that sex. This may not always be easy to do in the face of some circumstances in which parents may be on their own. Nevertheless, some ability to hold in mind the image of good relationships between men and women will be vital to the development of good relationships in children. At eleven, although most children will not be consciously aware of it, they will be gathering together their memories of this information and formulating their version of what sort of a woman or man they will be when they grow up. This information will contribute to what each child brings to the culture of their group.

It may be salutary for parents to observe the effects of their own attitudes to their partners on the attitudes and behavior of their children. Mothers who regard themselves as second-class citizens are not likely to provide much encouragement to their eleven-year-old daughters to grow up and join the ranks of women and mothers. Nor are they likely to be helpful to their sons' or daughters' attitudes if they only complain about their menfolk. Sons subjected to such complaints are not likely to feel enthusiastic about embarking on family life themselves. Fathers who insistently assert some sort of masculine superiority may well cause their sons to do likewise. Sons may, in the short run,

CHAPTER TWO

LOOKING FORWARD TO ADOLESCENCE

Eleven year-olds vary considerably one from another, as has been said, and in no respect more than the physical. In fact, it is probably their physical development that underlies many of their other differences. For many the changes of puberty will not be fully established for several years yet. Nevertheless, the beginnings of those changes will, for the great majority, begin to be felt. For girls, the twelfth year is a period of maximum growth, as hips begin to widen, and breasts become more apparent. The period of maximum growth is somewhat later for boys, but some secondary sexual characteristics, such as the filling out of the scrotum, often start developing at this age. Not all experts agree, but many are of the opinion that puberty changes start a year or so earlier for girls than for boys. Thus, one of the very important differences for the eleven year-old is that girls are much more in touch with sexual changes.

There is evidence to suggest that the age at which girls start to menstruate is getting progressively earlier. This is thought to be due to better nutrition and childcare. It is more difficult to identify the onset of puberty for boys but it is reasonable to assume that boys also become adolescent earlier. While the average girl would have started her periods at around fourteen in the earlier years of this century, nowadays that average is nearer twelve. Today eleven-year-old girls and boys will both today look forward to adolescence from much nearer the brink.

Physical changes in girls

Most girls start to develop breasts a bit before they are eleven. Their bodies will have begun to round out, their breasts to develop and pubic hair to show. Their hips will broaden and they will begin to shoot up in height. Few eleven-year-old girls will have reached their fully grown height, but some will be beginning to catch up to their mothers.

These changes in body will take some getting used to. In some ways these changes occur gradually, but in others, when girls begin to see that they are becoming as big as their mothers, it may have a marked effect on how they feel. Some may be disconcerted, still feeling quite young and wanting to be looked after by parents who they would like to look up to, literally. Others approximating more to their mothers in height may take this as a signal that they need take no further notice of what their mothers say, and forget their need to have access through grown-ups to a greater experience of life. Yet others may be really frightened of their increasing height and bodily changes, and may compensate by behaving in a more babyish way than they did before.

Whatever happens, it is certain that these changes will not pass unnoticed and that the eleven-year-old girl will in some way be responding to her changing physical status.

Physical changes in boys

There will be minimal changes in most boys during their twelfth year. However, their shoulders may begin to broaden, and their scrotum will enlarge. Few will have much of a growth spurt at this age, and while some may begin to approach their mothers in height, very few will be likely to overtake their fathers. Physically, it is likely that the eleven-year-old boy will continue to feel much the same as he has so far. Issues having to do with catching up with the grown-ups will be much less pressing than for girls, and the eleven-year-old boy can enjoy some increase in physical power without the experience of having to accommodate massive physical change.

Problems are more likely to arise from the opposite reason. Boys are preparing to grow taller, and those that are already below average in height may become more sensitive to this fact.

Ken was very little for his age. He had a hard life, and had suffered from undernourishment in his early years. It was very difficult for him, because he was the smallest in the school, and the senior boys and girls seemed to tower above him. Even the girls in his year were much bigger and seemed so much older. Ken was bright and had an appealing way with him and he soon became a bit of a pet ,especially with the more adolescent girls in his grade. He became popular, but in a way that he was not sure about. He felt grateful to the girls who looked after him in a motherly sort of way, passing him around between them as if he were a baby. But he also felt rather insulted that he was not given the respect that he felt was due to him at his age. Being so small he felt he needed their protection, but he wished it might be offered on different terms. His teacher noticed that he had become much more babyish than the previous year, when he had started to become more confident and independent. After a while, the girls tired of their relationship with Ken, and he became a bit sad and lonely and began to be bullied by some of the boys in his class. His art teacher, who had observed all this, also observed his isolation and the way some of the bigger boys were treating him. Ken was good at art and drawing and she encouraged him with this skill. The other children were impressed by his cartoons and portraits of the teachers and others in his class, including some telling pictures of those who bullied him, which they laughed at. As Ken's confidence grew he was again able to work effectively and to make friends with other boys and girls who disregarded his size. Eventually Ken nearly caught up with the others, but this experience helped him to realize that it is not how big you are but who you are that is important.

Puberty and the eleven-year-old girl

By eleven the average girl will have started to grow taller, and her breasts will have begun to develop. The clearest sign of sexual development is the first period for which the average age is twelve and a half. A substantial number of eleven-year-old girls will begin to menstruate. Their periods are quite likely to be irregular to begin with and full fertility will not be achieved immediately. It is not surprising to learn that research has shown that girls are more disturbed by the onset of puberty than boys. The sign of maturity—the menstrual blood—is clearly more disconcerting than equivalent ejaculations for boys. Girls who mature early, are likely to be more disconcerted than those who mature later and have seen their friends manage this watershed in their development. The younger the girl is, the fewer her resources and skills, the less is the experience she brings to this milestone. What will the young girl think about this sudden change in the behavior of her body?

Of course, it is enormously important that the eleven year-old is fully informed about the nature of the changes taking place in her body. Not so many years ago parents were too shy to tell their daughters the facts of life, including the facts of menstruation. Many an older woman will tell of the trauma of her first period, her feeling that she was damaged or suffering some awful illness. Some will have struggled, trying to disguise this, as they felt, shameful symptom from parents, who they thought would be worried. Even today, there are girls who are frightened of what is happening to them and do not want to accept their sexual maturity.

Doreen is an eleven year-old who was seriously sexually abused in her early childhood. She is now settled with an understanding foster-mother, who has been very helpful to her in her struggle with the effects of her early experience. Her foster-mother had told her about periods, but they started relatively early, when Doreen was just over eleven. Doreen, who was quite a tomboy, was horrified when her period started. She felt she was hopelessly damaged and asked her foster-mother to examine her to find the wound. To begin with she refused to wear any form of protection. She seemed to be convinced that if she ignored it, it would go away.

Doreen was a very unfortunate eleven year-old, whose life had made it difficult for her to accept things as they are. Her foster-mother had done everything she could to prepare her, but Doreen's fears and fantasies got the better of her in the face of this life event, which seemed like yet another trauma.

Not all girls are as dismayed by their sexual maturity as Doreen was. To many it is a sign that they are now more important and grown-up than they were before. This can be a mixed blessing for the eleven year-old, who will still retain many of the interests and characteristics she had when she was younger. Some will attempt to deal with it by becoming extra grown-up and sexy. Often their ideas of being grown-up will be rather artificial, based on ideas packaged in novels or seen on television—in fact a little-girl version of being grown-up. This is hardly surprising in the eleven year-old, but it may lead her into some unfortunate situations, and such an eleven year-old may need her parents to remind her that she has not done all her growing up yet.

Andrea was one such girl. She had never much liked being little and had always needed her parents to be firm and to remind her that she did not know it all yet. When her first period came early in her twelfth year, Andrea was very pleased, declaring her preference now for very high-heeled shoes and the latest fashions. She was scornful about doing her homework and about the other girls in her class with whom she used to be friends. She began to stay late after school, and not come home for supper, though she always had before. Her mother became worried, and was even more so when she saw Andrea out with a particular group of girls from high school, girls of thirteen and fourteen. Andrea was not as sophisticated as she would have liked to have been, and her friendship with these girls was short-lived. She couldn't keep up with them and was rather frightened by some of the experiments they were trying. She was sick after her first few puffs at a cigarette. She could not keep up with her new friends, and soon returned to the girls of her own age who she knew better. One by one they caught up with her and their periods started, and Andrea could join in with the gradual development that most securely brings a girl into adolescence. Andrea's parents managed not to allow their anxiety to get the better of them. They gently insisted she do her homework and come home sensibly, but they also knew that this was a difficult moment for her and trusted in her good sense.

Doreen and Andrea were girls who started their periods rather early. What of the majority who still, at eleven, are not menstruating? Most will carry on as usual in the knowledge that, sooner or later, they will start as well. Some may be relieved. Others may be a bit worried, anxiously waiting to catch up with the girl in the next desk, scrutinizing themselves for signs of maturing. Books like *What's Happening to My Body?* by Lynda Madaras can be very helpful, indicating the stages in sexual development, by which the adolescent can chart her way forward.

The sexual development of boys

On the whole, boys weather puberty with greater ease than girls. This is hardly surprising as the physical changes entailed are fewer and, on the whole, boys experience them later, and therefore on the basis of greater experience. It is more difficult to estimate the age at which boys first mature. A girl's first period is more noticeable than a boy's first nocturnal emission. The increase in scrotum and penis size, and the development of pubic hair are essentially more private than the changes that can be witnessed in the maturing girl. Nevertheless, some boys may experience a quickening of sexual interest, and masturbation, which most have practiced hitherto, may become more persistent.

It will be the rare eleven year-old who will be experiencing any marked hormonal change. Those who do will probably be taller and stronger than their friends, and will, as such, be at quite an advantage over the others in their class. Such boys will be making more contact with the girls in their class and will probably appear more grown-up in their work and interests. In being stronger physically, such boys may enjoy a period of high status among the others; some may be self-conscious about their development and try to hide it by stooping and hoping to look smaller. On the whole, however, well-grown boys are happy to be as they are, and are able to turn it to good use socially.

Eating and sleeping

Even if eleven year-olds are not yet pubescent, they will be looking forward to this next stage, growing or preparing to grow. With this in prospect, eating and sleeping are very important. You may find that your eleven year-old has a very healthy appetite, and also a desire to sleep in in the morning. With the eleven year-old, gone are the days when parents would be wakened at dawn by children wanting to be up and doing; many eleven year-olds are difficult to get going in the morning and may also be difficult to get to bed at night. Growing is a tiring business and eleven year-olds doing it may need help with establishing sensible habits that will stand them in good stead in later life.

It is not just in eating and sleeping that eleven year-olds need help towards good habits. By eleven, most should be looking after themselves, washing their own hair, cutting their nails, keeping themselves clean and regularly cleaning their teeth. Not all eleven-year-old boys are interested in cleanliness. They may need occasional (or not so occasional) reminders from parents. But it is important that these routines are established by this age, and that they are reinforced by example within the family. It is much more difficult to insist when the child has moved into adolescence. The eleven year-old can still be reminded and these routines once well established will reassert themselves eventually, even if they become matter for rebellion in the course of adolescence.

Most eleven year-olds have hearty appetites and may not always choose the most wholesome food—chocolate, potato chips and hamburgers may be their preferred meals. But few have serious eating problems, and those that have are probably girls and are likely to be among the more sexually advanced. Boys who have difficulties about eating are likely to be children with long-standing problems in this respect and their parents have probably been seeking medical advice about them for some years. It is not common for boys to have no wish to eat.

Some girls do, around adolescence, start to diet because they feel too fat. Anorexia is a serious disorder, if a child stops eating in a major way. The reasons for this failure to eat are complex, and will include the girl's relation ship both with herself and her family. She may not wish to develop into an adolescent and the members of her family may have their own reasons for agreeing with her and for not helping her to grow up. The result may be a child who has difficulty in eating, a difficulty that is made worse by its physical consequences, once her refusal to eat is established.

Fortunately, it is a rare condition among eleven year-olds. It is much more likely that parents will be worried about its opposite, as their children stuff themselves with junk food and begin to put on some puppy fat. Some parents may, at this point, wonder whether their daughters need to diet. Some girls may indeed be devouring quite inappropriate amounts of food. However, parents might wonder why this is so, before leaping into action and imposing dietary restrictions.

At eleven, Jody had filled out a bit, though her periods had not begun. Her mother became worried when Jody got really pudgy, and noticed that not only did Jody eat heartily at all meals, but was seldom to be seen without a candy bar or a bag of potato chips. Things to eat seemed to absorb all her pocket money. Jody's dad also noticed the changes. She was no longer the slim attractive child she used to be but was a little butterball. Dad had lost his job and had just started a training course, Mom had gone to work full-time to support the family, and Jody's elder brother was working in a store after school to help out for the time being. Jody's weight, however, became such a worry to her mother that she felt she had to talk about it with her husband even at the cost of worrying him further. As they talked, it became clear to them that Jody had started to put on weight at the beginning of that school year. At first they wondered if it had to do with changes at school, from more practical work to subjects like math, history and geography. Jody didn't seem much interested in school work these days. Then Mom realized that the weight gain also dated from the time when Jody had to come home from school to an empty house. Jody's brother was at the store, her mother now worked till six o'clock and her father tended to stay on at the college, doing extra work in the hope of ultimately improving his job prospects. Sometimes Jody went out to a friend's, but mostly she came home to watch television—and eat.

Previously she had come in, perhaps with a friend, talked with her mom who had helped with any project she was doing at school, or perhaps they had gone to meet her dad after work. Sometimes Jody and her brother had played a bit. Now, it seemed to Jody's parents, there might be a big gap in her life that had previously been filled by family activities. This gap was now being filled by food. Her parents had been so concerned with their own problems they had not noticed the effect of these problems on Jody, or what she was doing to cheer herself up. Jody's dad decided he might come home a bit earlier to be there for his daughter. Jody's mom, instead of nagging about Jody's overeating, started providing low-calorie meals for everybody and managed to find time to help Jody with her homework. Little by little Jody began to lose the pounds she had put on, comforting herself for what had seemed like the loss of her close family life.

Jody's parents did not chide or tease her about being too fat. If they had done that they might have put her on the path to over-dieting. Nagging her about her homework might have made things worse. Instead, they stopped and thought about her, and not just her, but all of them. They realized that her eating was making up for something she felt she had lost—their attention and concern. Once she was settled into the changes at school, she and her dad worked together in the evening. Her mom could go back to the domestic chores she had to do on her return from work, and the whole family returned to their ordinary diet. Jody gave up over-eating and resumed her normal development.

When parents notice changes like this, it is a good idea to think about what is going on. Often it seems easier to attack the presenting worry or symptom than to wonder why the worry comes up now and whether it

CHAPTER THREE

YOUR ELEVEN YEAR-OLD IN THE FAMILY

Sometimes parents mistake the extent of the independence of the eleven year-old, and imagine that they are more able to look after themselves than, in fact, they are. One eleven year-old was left on her own in the somewhat distant care of an elderly neighbor, while her mother, who needed the money, went off to work for two weeks. All went reasonably well, until the neighbor fell ill. The girl had got herself to school each day, seeming clean and tidy, a little upset perhaps, but apparently all right. She could just about keep going until the neighbor fell ill. Then, she collapsed at school, and other arrangements had to be made for her. Not all eleven year-olds could have managed as much but it seems clear that this girl could take care of herself to a considerable extent. But not completely it seems, and this illustrates the position of the eleven year-old very well.

Some eleven year-olds may seem to be on the threshold of being able to look after themselves, but, in fact they still need grown-ups—their parents or others—if not physically, at least emotionally, as a support. The great majority of eleven year-olds are very far from being able to look after themselves as well as this girl did.

But the dilemma is there. An eleven year-old may appear to him or herself, and to others, to have gained a lot of competence in managing life but this competence is still very new, if it exists at all. Just as when children begin to be able to play by themselves, and to begin to move away from their caregiver—parent or nursery teacher—they keep needing to refer back to them, to know a grown-up is still there with an eye on them, so at eleven the growing person really needs to know his or her parents are there and at least thinking about him or her.

Most eleven year-olds are cheerfully able to leave their parents for holiday periods, perhaps staying with grandparents, or going off for a few days with school or to holiday camps. They will have developed a good enough memory of loving and reliable parents to sustain them through periods without these particular grown-ups. If they can remember home and parents, they will almost certainly expect those others in the family to remember them and to be interested and awaiting their return. It is this capacity to remember, and hold in mind those who are not with them, that enables eleven year-olds to stay away from home for a while and look forward to new experiences. This applies not just to going away on vacation, but also to other unfamiliar occasions.

The ability to separate from one's family is often well established by the age of eleven, but the ease with which this is accomplished is somewhat dependent on the sorts of memories that the child holds in mind. Also important is whether the child feels held in mind by the family, and cared for by the adults with whom he or she now is. Eleven year-olds may sometimes feel they are not being thought about, when in fact, they are.

Sandra, for example, was used to going away with her family, her mom and dad and older brother. They were a close family and, on the whole, did things together. Mostly her dad worked near home, but he was sent away on a job for a few days near to where her mom used to live, and where a very old friend still lived. So her mom decided to join her dad. It was the middle of the school term and since Sandra was now eleven, it was decided that while her parents were away, Sandra would stay with some friends whom she knew well. Her brother, also, was going to stay with friends who lived near to where Sandra would be. Sandra was cross at being left behind; she was not as independent and grown-up-seeming as the girl who was referred to at the beginning of the chapter and she wanted to go with her parents. Her parents did their best to prepare her for these few days apart, but Sandra felt aggrieved and cried when it was time for her parents to go. Her mother was upset and telephoned each night. This helped quite a bit, but Sandra found it difficult to concentrate at school. She wished she didn't have to go to school. At home with her friends, she did her best and over these few days began to establish some trust with her friend's parents, whom she normally liked a lot. Nevertheless it was a very problematic visit. Sandra was not yet able to manage without her family and her wish that she was with them got in the way of her enjoying a new experience. Her older brother had a more satisfactory time, and perhaps Sandra will too, when she is older.

Eleven year-olds are growing up, and may well feel quite big by that age, but in most cultures, they still need their parents to go on being parental. However they may not be as willing to accept adult guidance and discipline as they used to be. The problem for those looking after an eleven year-old is how not to squash their burgeoning independence while providing a framework of living in which they can feel secure.

Eleven year-olds and their mothers

The growing independence of eleven year-olds can present problems, particularly, in their relationship with their mothers. Mothers, or others in this role, have, after all, looked after their eleven year-olds for all the previous years, from the time when they had to do more or less everything for them. So it is hardly surprising if it is sometimes difficult for them to realize how much their children have grown. Of course, this is true for mothers and children of all ages, but it is a particularly sensitive issue for many eleven year-olds—and mothers may feel it more than other members of the family. Moreover, as puberty draws nearer, sexual awareness begins to complicate all the relationships within the family. The combination both of dawning sexuality and of independence may make the twelfth year a tricky one for mothers as their children draw away from them and begin to want to settle their own affairs.

It may be especially difficult for the single parent who may have come to rely on a close relationship with his or her child, as he or she begins to move away.

Mothers and sons

The situation may differ depending on the sex of the child. Boys, beginning to feel more masculine, may feel more and more need to assert themselves. They may now take more notice of their dads and seem to draw away from their mom with never a backward glance. They may start to reject quite a lot of what their mother has stood for in the past and may refuse to continue to carry out washing, teeth cleaning and other domestic tasks, which they have been happy to perform in the past as part of a co-operative relationship with their mother. Too much closeness may make such a boy feel smaller than he wants to feel, and also threatened physically. He may over-react in the other direction.

Fathers and male partners can often be a great help in the management of such problems, setting an example of how to be both independent and considerate. They can also assist with those important aspects of life that have up to now been the mother's province alone, thus indicating that there are things that it is appropriate both for men and women to do without distinction. The relationship between partners is, of course, closely observed by children of all ages and provides a vital basis for the child's appreciation of how people in general relate to each other, and in particular, how men and women get on together. But it is never more important than for the eleven-year-old boy, who is just starting to be able to think realistically of how he wants to be when he is grown-up.

But what of the single mother, with no partner there to take over sometimes and to allow the boy to work out his relation with the other partner? The single mother may have to find a way of maintaining a *parental* relationship with her son, while appreciating that he may need to grow away from her as the one who has looked after him in intimate ways for so long. In matters of discipline, this can be quite a problem, but also in other ways it can be an anxious business, watching the child move away on his own, and hoping he will be able to manage by himself. Parents, of course, have to do this progressively throughout the child's life—as he toddles away, and then as he goes to school—but the choices for the mother of an eleven year-old may be even more taxing.

Tony lived with his mother and his small sister. He had developed a group of friends at his school that his mother did not really know, because the school was quite a distance from his home. Sometimes these friends went to play at the house of one of the group, and Tony's mom was happy to let him do that, provided he told her where he was and when he would be home. But one day, he came home asking to be allowed to go with them to the city high school championship football game. She was not quite sure what to do about this. In some ways she felt he was old and responsible enough to go, but she worried about the roughness and excitability of the crowd and whether the boys could really look after themselves. She wished Tony's father could take him, which she felt would have been the answer, at least to begin with, to show him the ropes. But his father was out of the country. She could not go, and she knew he would find her presence far too embarrassing. She wondered what to do. Rescue came to her in the shape of her young brother, who lived in a nearby town. He had got in touch wanting to make one of his occasional visits, and she persuaded him to come as soon as he could, and to ask Tony whether he could come along to the game. Her brother was acceptably able to keep an eye on the young football fans and also to reassure her that the boys would be likely to be all right in the future.

By taking time to think, and with a bit of luck, Tony's mother was able to preserve his feeling of growing up, and also to contain her own understandable anxiety.

Mothers and daughters

Despite the fact that most girls at this age will be nearer to puberty than most boys, the relationship between mother and daughter may be a bit less problematic than that between mother and son. Later on, mothers and daughters become more rivalrous, and in some cases they may always have been, but girls need their mothers to show them about life and growing up. Girls may want and be able at eleven to demonstrate their independence (like the girl mentioned at the beginning of the chapter), but they also know they have a lot to learn. Eleven-year-old girls may want quite a sisterly relationship with their mothers, and may find themselves shopping and talking together more like contemporaries.

Some mothers may really welcome this development in their relationship with their daughters. It may have been what they had wanted with their own mothers and had, perhaps, never been able to achieve. They may enjoy with their daughter the feeling of being again on the threshold of life. However, there can be difficulties in negotiating the two roles, the one of being a friend to their daughter and at the same time having still to be a parent, with a longer view of life and with all that means in terms of saying "no" sometimes. Eleven year-olds still sometimes need discipline and parents to take responsibility, which will mean curbing some of the child's feelings, wishes and aspirations. If mothers of children of this age are too sisterly, they may lose their authority and with it the stance from which to offer the grown-up vision and support that is needed. Eleven year-olds are not helped by feeling that they are already grown-up and that they can take full responsibility for themselves and their decisions. If they feel too big for their boots they will certainly be difficult to manage. So mothers tempted to be over-sisterly with their daughters may pay for it with fights and defiance when their eleven year-olds demonstrate they don't know everything after all and need correcting.

Gloria and her mother lived together and had done so since her father had left when Gloria was very small. They were very close and Gloria had always resented it if her mother had any other relationship. It was a relief to her mother when Gloria had begun to grow up and they could begin to share interests a bit more. Everyone said they seemed like sisters and this pleased both of them. Gloria felt grown-up and important. Gloria's mother felt she must still look young, attractive and full of life. Gloria started wanting to stay up with her mother at night until quite late. Why should she go to bed before her mom? she demanded. Her mother was somewhat swayed by this argument and, wishing to maintain an amicable relationship, gave in. Gloria wanted to go to bed later and later and also began to refuse to get up in the morning. She started to be late for school and she became cross and tired. Her mother, too, began to get cross with Gloria, but there seemed to be no way to intervene and help Gloria to return to a more harmonious way of life at home and at school. Certainly getting cross did not work, but led to more and more rebellion.

Gloria's work at school was also suffering and she was in serious trouble with it. Gloria's mom got fed up and could no longer maintain her sisterly attitude. She began to feel she did not want to go out with

Gloria and found herself adopting a more parental role. But it was difficult to manage this and insist that Gloria did what she was told. In some ways it was rather fortunate that she was in trouble at school, for before long, Gloria's mother was called to meet her teacher and principal. Between them they worked out a regime for Gloria who would have to report to her teacher each morning before school with her homework done. Her mother, supported by the school, had good reason to insist on early nights and relatively early rising. It took time and a great deal of kind firmness all around, but Gloria was able to return to behavior more ordinary for an eleven year-old.

Gloria's mom had nearly let her wish for a friendly relationship with her daughter get out of hand. It required some effort and a co-operative school to restore Gloria to her right size, or rather her right age. But the effort was well worth it. Both could then pursue their lives in their own age-appropriate ways, while staying reasonably harmoniously together.

Fathers and sons

Fathers and sons may find themselves moving a little closer together during their son's twelfth year as he starts to approach puberty. As we saw in Tony's case, many boys may be overseen more easily by fathers in some circumstances than by mothers. Fathers should savor this precious time, because once adolescence really gets going, they will nearly always lose their influence. It is important, at this time, that sons are helped not to enter a male alliance against mothers and sisters, but instead to be helped to see that differences are to be recognized and valued. They can then have a chance of moving into adolescence with a positive view of the other sex. This goes for both sexes and alliances between mothers and daughters and girls and their sisters against fathers and brothers can be equally destructive of their long-term relationships. This is a time of life when fathers and sons can do things together and share interests. Fathers can help their sons to enjoy life before the boy begins to assert his independence from the whole family. Many fathers and sons have for a long time enjoyed these sorts of relationships, but by the time the son is eleven he can contribute more and may need a bit less from his dad. Wise dads will recognize this and find ways of fostering the boys' developing skills and fresh vision of what is shared with their fathers. If fathers and sons have not had such relationships before, it might be a good moment to try again.

Of course, many dads may not be in such a fortunate position, either because other commitments limit their time with their sons or because they do not live with the family. Boys of this age may be very sensitive to the absence of their fathers, as they begin to move away from their earlier dependent relationship with the mother and, needing someone else, may be angrier and more difficult with absent fathers than before. Such boys will, with any luck, move into more comfortable relationships with both parents in due course, a hope that may sustain a father with limited time for his son, through what could otherwise be a difficult stage.

Fathers and daughters

How fathers and daughters get along will depend, as for all the other combinations of parents and children, on how relationships have developed over previous years. The relationship of the eleven-year-old girl with her dad will also be affected by the extent to which she is nearing adolescence. Some eleven-year-old girls can go on being the same little girl for their dads that they have always been. Others, sensing more immediately their developing sexuality will become much more sensitive to a new dimension in their dealings with their fathers. Fathers are, from the very first, a model of how men are for their children. As the girl grows into a woman, she looks to her father as the first man to respond to her sexuality. Most fathers can trust themselves to respond appropriately to their growing daughters, appreciating and encouraging them while maintaining a parental position. A few may feel unduly threatened and may withdraw from their adolescent daughters or become over-stimulated and over-stimulating. Yet others may become disapproving of their daughter's adolescent experiments. While disapproval may be in order some times, it should be remembered that times change and that too much disapproval may cause rebellion, which is usually counter-productive, or may inhibit the girl's attempts to work things out for herself. Over-reaction of any sort may complicate the development of the daughter and could cause widespread family complications, which may, in turn, hold back the daughter's growing up. Fathers experiencing difficulty with their daughter's maturing can draw comfort from the fact that this is a common state of affairs, while needing, nevertheless, to monitor and think about their own disturbing reactions to it.

Marie's mother had died a couple of years before her eleventh birthday, leaving Marie alone with her father. They had mourned together and clung together, striving to keep their little family going. Marie's dad's work as a teacher enabled him to come home more or less when she did after school and in the evenings they worked together; she at the homework she was assigned, while he did his marking. On holidays they went to a trailer park by the ocean, sometimes on their own and sometimes joining friends who had a trailer near them. They continued the life that they had established when Marie's mother was alive. This way of life continued for a while, until Marie began to develop physically. Her periods started in her twelfth year. She was a pretty girl, whose maturing body showed promise that she would become a very attractive young woman. To his horror her father found her just that. She began to notice the effect she was having on older boys and to notice a somewhat similar quality in her father's response to her. She was both flattered and alarmed and did not know how to respond herself. Could she be as she used to be, her father's affectionate daughter still? There seemed to be a different quality about it these days. Her father, without his own sexual relationship, was equally disquieted and their relationship became anxious and irritable.

The long summer holidays loomed ahead. For the first time neither felt happy to go to the trailer park, though neither felt able to express their worries except by being cross with each other. Feeling a bit desperate, the father phoned the mother of the family in the trailer next door. Were they going to be there this summer? Fortunately they were, and Marie's father began to feel a little happier and more relaxed. Marie was able to relax in response. During the summer holiday Marie went off with her friends while her father gradually began to talk to his neighbors of his worries about his closeness to his daughter. They could reassure him about how usual his feelings were, while at the same time helping him to look at the need to find a life of his own away from his daughter's and for her to find hers with her own friends. Talking to trusted friends can be a great help to parents and children alike. Marie's dad, beginning to get over the period of mourning for his wife, was able to think about what he was feeling and, putting it into perspective, could use his feelings and these discussions to review his life and put their relationship back on track.

Fathers, as well as representing to their children what it is like to be a man, may also be in touch with different aspects of the world outside the family. Mothers are sometimes preoccupied with domestic responsibilities, and father can present another and special view. Fathers who are interested in their daughters' school work can find here a useful way to relate to them and value them. Shared interests of these kinds can provide a useful balance for the more sensitive aspects of the daughter's sexual development. Fathers who can achieve a balanced and harmonious relationship with their daughters will contribute importantly to their future relationships.

Parental difficulties

How will the eleven year-old respond if all is not well between his parents? The eleven year-old will be just as torn and upset as a child of any other age, but by now will be sensitive to the tension and sadness that the grown-ups will be experiencing as well. It is always much more of a problem to manage the upset experienced by children when parents themselves are upset. Parents may want to protect the children from their own distress, but it is seldom possible to do so and less and less possible as children grow older. If children are not told what is going on, they will find their own explanations for what they observe. These imagined explanations are usually more alarming and highly colored than what is, in fact, happening, and it is often a relief if children can be calmly told the straight facts. This is particularly true for the child of this age, whose knowledge of life and capacity to think and talk about it means that parents can talk, and expect to be understood, in ways that have not before been possible. This does not mean that the child will not be distressed, but that the distress can be more contained than can that of the younger child. Telling the child will take a great deal of calm, as will patiently managing the response, but it will be well worth doing in order that all concerned can weather this taxing time in the family's life.

Step-parents

Step-parents who are well established with their eleven-year-old step-children will find little different in their relationships during this period. Relationships with step-parents are often more intense, particularly where negative reactions are concerned. Step-children may overreact and assert their independence more strongly from step-mothers than from their natural mothers, but given that there is a general tenor of good relationships and openness, step-parents can expect "business as usual" more often than not at this stage.

If single parents of an eleven year-old are considering remarriage or moving in with a new partner, again, general principles of openness and discussion are of more importance than the particular age of the child. The eleven year-old is much more capable of observing what is going on and talking about it than when younger, and any secrets or things kept hidden are now likely to be more disturbing. If a single parent is thinking of changing his or her single status, and is *not* telling the child, it will not be surprising if trouble ensues. The eleven year-old will be more sensitive than ever to being left out and not thought grown-up enough to know. They may react with distress when things are going on that they only half understand, and when they cannot help knowing that parents are involved in something which they have not been told about. At eleven, such difficulties are compounded by the insult to the growing maturity and intelligence that the child of that age experiences.

If the eleven year-old knows what is going on, and time is allowed for all the parties to get to know each other, the children will cope with their mixed feelings (which the parental partners may *not* be feeling at this time). In that case, this age should not be any more difficult for negotiating such changes than any other, and indeed may be easier than some.

Brothers and sisters

If relationships with brothers and sisters change it will probably have as much to do with the sibling as with the eleven year-old. For example, an eleven year-old with a much admired elder brother or sister who is in the middle of some sort of adolescent turmoil may well be more affected by it than a younger child. In such a situation, the eleven year-old might react either by siding more than ever with the adolescent, or may

45

go to the other extreme by regressing to behavior of an even earlier kind, to increase the difference between them. Sometimes the eleven year-old, flushed with the importance of dawning maturity, may wish to emphasize this by moving away from a close relationship with a younger child, but, as has been said many times before, eleven year-olds are so different from one another that, equally, the opposite might happen.

Children of this age, however, are becoming more aware of their position in the world, and also within the family. Rani and Mary, the two friends in Chapter One, were just such cases.

Billy's work at school suddenly fell off when he was eleven. This was a worry because he was due to change school, and the new school wanted to know how he was likely to perform in various subjects, so that he could be placed among children of similar ability. His work in most subjects had been good until recently, but then it had started to change. Further inquiry revealed that his younger brother, who had been diagnosed as having special educational needs, was being placed in a special class. Billy was very aware of this and for a variety of reasons, having to do at least partly with his own change of school, had lost confidence in his own ability. Once the school had spoken with the parents and realized how upset Billy was about his brother, both could help Billy to recognize the difference of his position and help him not to sabotage his own prospects. It took a bit of time but ultimately Billy caught up and began to do justice to himself. And it was important for him to do so, and for him to recognize that failing himself was no help to his brother, and that in fact fulfilling himself gave him greater opportunities to help him.

Grandparents

Grandparents may be very helpful with the eleven year-old, or they may not. It all depends whether they are able to keep up and recognize how their grandchildren are growing or whether they carry on treating them as they always have. And of course, the older we get, the more difficult it is to keep up with changes. If, however, grandparents respond flexibly to the new capabilities of their eleven-year-old grandchildren, they can provide a comfortable way station on their journey towards adolescence. Grandparents can, for example, have their grandchildren to stay, providing somewhat familiar surroundings for them to practice being on their own or, at least, without those who know them best. Moreover, grandparents who can keep pace with the children's development can offer a familiar person with whom to discuss and put into words feelings and uncertainties about the world. Children can share with them their inner thoughts and fantasies of what it is all about. Grandparents need not be as formidable as the parental generation, whom they meet not just as parents, but also, for example, as teachers, policemen, shopkeepers and sports coaches.

The other major role for grandparents at this, or any other stage, is that of keeping the whole family in mind. It is a vital role of enabling the whole family to know that whatever they do, Grandmother and Grandfather are interested and that they care. Grandparents who can do this and who can provide the knowledge of their ongoing concern for their children and their children's children (their grandchildren) will fulfill an important function for everybody, and will find adapting to an eleven-year-old grandchild just part of the job.

Eleven year-olds need to feel safe within the context of their relationships with all their family, grandparents, siblings, mothers and fathers, because they are likely to be facing major changes in their working life, at school.

CHAPTER FOUR

YOUR ELEVEN YEAR-OLD AT SCHOOL

Around eleven your child's ways of thinking change. Whereas when children were eight and nine they were practical and needing to try things out for themselves in order to learn and understand, around eleven they start to think and learn for themselves by using their minds in a more logical way. Your eleven year-old draws on memory to develop an argument, a capacity that increases during adolescence and continues through life.

This capacity to think in more abstract ways does not suddenly come into being at eleven. Some children are more advanced when younger, and some lag behind. Most, however, are well on their way by eleven and this results in some major changes. It is, perhaps, what contributes to the greater independence noticeable in your eleven year-old, and apparent in their family relationships. They have a developing independence of mind. This is why it is more possible to explain family difficulties and discuss plans with them than previously. This is why they can contribute more to shared interests, and why their reading interests change from stories with straightforward plots to more complex books that explore human relationships and situations. The eleven year-old can start to think about thinking itself.

Changes at school

Nowhere are these changes more noticeable than at school. In years gone by the young child of seven, eight and nine was taught by rote and learned reading, writing and arithmetic. But then it was found that while these children might be able to recite all of these academic facts, they did not wholly understand them. New methods of teaching were evolved by which these principles were absorbed as parts of practical exercises and projects involving doing things, so that not just the mere facts were learned but they were understood in application.

Teachers and schools differ a great deal in the extent to which early learning is practical or more theoretical, but nearly every school includes some individual use of materials for children of eight and nine. By the time their pupils are eleven a more academic program is almost always adopted—less project work, more learning of subjects like history, geography, science and languages. These subjects require the child to think and imagine and reason rather than to try out by doing. In this manner educators acknowledge the changes in the way children of eleven and over use their minds.

Not all children develop at the same rate. For some children these changes at school can pose a considerable threat. Yet others have been ready for a long time and may have found their own ways of moving on—either in the quality of their work or in the use of their leisure time. Most children, however, will be more or less ready to undertake academic work more seriously around eleven years old and will be prepared to go along with the changes in the system designed to accommodate them at this stage.

With this in mind it is important that children have by eleven mastered the basic skills in reading, writing and math. It is easy to miss out on some of these necessary skills due to illness or other reasons for absence from school. Basic skills build up one upon the other. For example, it is not possible to do more complicated multiplication if you are unable to add, or to divide if subtraction is not mastered. Children can be held back in ways that are often complicated to understand. From eleven, children move on to more and more applications of their basic skills. It is important that these skills are at their finger-tips.

Steven's dad was in the armed forces and he had moved around quite a bit. Steven therefore had been to a number of different schools. When Steven was eleven his dad left the Forces and the family settled in one place. Steven's younger sister made the change to a new school very easily and was delighted to know she was going to stay there. Steven was not so happy. He made friends quickly as usual, but he was very restless, could not concentrate and hated the work. His friends tended to be boys who also did not want to work. Steven's parents became worried about his new school. The way in which work was presented had changed very considerably from what he was used to. Previously lessons had been organized in an open way; children had worked at their own pace in small groups, and Steven had grown accustomed to asking other children for help if he could not manage what he was asked to do. Things were not like this in his new school. Different subjects were taught by different teachers. While some subjects, like science, were still practical, in others, such as history and English, he had to sit still, listen to the teacher and do a lot of reading and writing. Steven's mom and dad were worried about his dislike of the work in his new school, and so were his teachers. His teachers, considering what he could and could not do, wondered whether Steven's basic skills were as strong as they should be given that he seemed to be a bright boy. His arithmetic was all right and his writing was very neat, but he seemed very slow to learn when he had to read. His teacher wondered whether his reading was good enough. His parents were struck by this, and added that Steven was never to be found at home with his nose in a book. A brief test by the educational psychologist revealed that Steven was, in fact, below his age and ability in reading. Some help for him was prescribed and his parents were also shown how they could do more for him at home. It took time for Steven to catch up what he had missed in all his changes of school. Once he felt he could keep up with the reading work, Steven began to enjoy his new subjects at school and then could settle down.

Steven was lucky—it did not take much to bring his skills up to a level that was usable at school. Others are not so fortunate, and their problems will be discussed later in more detail. There are many children who find the changes in academic work around eleven difficult to adjust to. Parents may have to allow for the inevitable anxieties that arise and offer sympathetic support.

Changes of school

Steven changed school at eleven because his father moved to a new job. Children have grown to be less dependent on their surroundings and by now, as has been discussed above, they are ready for rather different teaching styles. Steven's parents, when they thought they were going to continue to move around, had even wondered about boarding school. They had thought he might be able to manage on his own in a community of children looked after by caring adults, and were probably right. Eleven is a bit young for children to go to boarding school, but it is an age at which some could manage temporary separations from parents if it were necessary. Steven's parents discussed the possibility with him and he was very excited by the prospect, being confident that he would get along well with the other children. Many children might not have been so confident and could have suffered from such an early separation from their family. In any event Steven's circumstances did not make this necessary.

Moving to a new school is bound to cause some disruption for a child. But a lot can be done before they start and in careful selection of the new school. The more the children who are coming to the new school know about it, the more confident they will feel.

The choice of school is a critical matter. Parents have to balance the nearness of the school with its reputation. Many schools offer potential students and their parents opportunities to visit the school and to find out about it. Parents will need to consider not only academic standards and whether these suit their child, but arrangements for attention to particular needs of their pupils, including arrangements for new children.

Homework, exams, report cards

Children vary a great deal, as we have said in Chapter One, in the ways in which they handle changes of teaching methods. As well as the nature of the new work, there may be a considerable increase in the amount of independent work that children are expected to do. In particular, they may be required to do homework. How much will be demanded each night, and whether it has been required before the child is eleven, will vary a lot from school to school. Parents may wonder how to manage this new or increased requirement. It is important to find out how much work the child is likely to have to do each night and what facilities there are for finishing homework within the school day. Are there free periods available for doing the assigned independent work or is the child likely to have to do it all at home? Armed with this information you will then know how much of an eye you should keep on what is to be done at home.

Homework is set to enable children to work more independently, so parents only need to keep a distant eye on the work that is done at home. However, at first some children may need help in organizing themselves, and assisting them to do this can play an important part in showing children how to manage themselves. Parents who take little interest in how their children manage their work may find that their children have little interest in it either.

Some children may be prepared to come straight home from school and settle down to their work, getting it over with quickly so they can be free for their own concerns afterwards. Parents may feel they rush headlong through it, taking too little care. Other children may seem to come in from school exhausted and need snacks and television in order to unwind and recover before sitting down to homework. Parents may fear that such children may go on putting it off, and that it may never get done. Your anxieties on both accounts may be entirely justified, but when the child has a prescribed amount of homework to do, you may find it best to leave it to the school to monitor whether the child is organizing it success fully. If, after a term or so, the school complains of inadequate work, then it may be time for you to intervene. School and home working together is always more effective. Parents too closely overseeing the child's work can run the risk of making school and homework a subject for their child's later adolescent rebellion. If you can maintain a sympathetic interest without interference you are likely to be more helpful to the eleven year-old in establishing good work habits.

The same goes for actively helping with the child's assignments. Some children are quite successful in pressing their parents actually to work out their math or contribute to the essay they are supposed to write. One mother was disappointed in only getting a B+ for a piece of work that her daughter should have done, but which she had got roped into completing. If children have parents who contribute too much to their work they lose their capacity to do it themselves. On the other hand just leaving work to the child, without showing interest, may communicate to the child that school work is not worth serious attention. You can find your own way towards a balance between encouragement of your child's work and active participation in it. If the balance can be struck at around eleven, when homework issues have just become crucial, this will provide a useful support for children throughout their school careers.

Homework is not the only aspect of school life that achieves prominence for the eleven year-old; they may be seriously confronted with set examinations at the end of term as well. All children will have had some experience of tests before eleven, but many children in their twelfth year will for the first time sit in a room with their classmates to answer questions on their term's work unaided and in a given time. How each child will respond to this situation will depend very much on their confidence in their work. If they have understood what they have been taught, and if they feel supported by parents who understand their strengths and weaknesses, and if they do not expect perfection of themselves, they will be able to take this new situation in their stride. Some whose work habits have not enabled them to really digest what they have been taught and who feel unsure of their learning, may be more anxious. Also some who are afraid of the consequences of not doing well, either because of parental disapproval or because they cannot bear to fail, may be very worried. Such children may become anxious or panicky and may not do their best. People can get worried about exams at any time in their lives, particularly if the results are important for the candidate's future. However, as with homework, if eleven year-olds can feel relaxed and confident at the start of their examination careers, it will enable them to meet later challenges more easily.

For many eleven year-olds grades may become much more important. For instance there are almost certain to be more subject reports as well as reports from more teachers. Your response to these reports—as indeed to many aspects of the school life of your children—may be colored by your own experience. Parents who were themselves, for example, pressured into being good performers at school may in turn have the same expectations of their children. Such parents may find it hard to be encouraging when their children encounter difficulties in their work. If they themselves had parents who fastened on the deficiencies in their report cards as if to drive them to further effort, they may be unable to encourage their own children by responding to the good comments as well as the bad, and by noting the small changes when their child has tried a little harder. Many children dread taking their report cards home because their failures seem to arouse more attention than their successes. As with homework and exams, if you can offer measured encouragement and support, not enthusing too much over success, nor over-emphasizing difficulties but sympathetically helping your child to tackle what problems there may be, then, again, your child will be helped to have a relaxed enjoyment in the work.

Special needs

All children have to take in their stride the intellectual changes that take place as a part of ordinary growing up. For some it is more difficult. These are the ones for whom school life at the age of eleven can be a particular strain. Such children may have been able to get by when academic work was easier and more practical and the circumstances of learning, in one classroom with one main teacher, were easier. Steven, spoken of earlier in this chapter, had managed to conceal his problems about reading until he was eleven. A bright boy, he had got by through observing the other children and talking with them. He had even been able to bluff his way through individual reading sessions. Many other children are supported through their early schooling by familiar teachers and pupils. However, if your child has difficulties that need special attention, it is helpful if they can be identified at least by the time your child is eleven. Your child can then make use of the special facilities that are usually available to help.

Children who are struggling with special difficulties often make their needs known by awkward and disruptive behavior in class. It is possible that some children derive satisfaction and a feeling of importance from upsetting a lesson and causing confusion to teachers and classmates, but for the vast majority, such behavior is more of a sign that the child is experiencing some distress in his or her own right.

Janet was always whispering to her friend at the back of the class, and this was very annoying. Teachers had not been told that Janet suffered from a degree of deafness and could not properly hear what was being said. Moving both Janet and her friend to the front of all classes quickly dealt with what might have developed into a major problem.

Specific learning disabilities

Other problems are less simply resolved. Some children's difficulties in reading and writing are based in perceptual problems, and difficulties in remembering sequences of numbers or letters. Such children are often confused about which way letters are written, reversing b's and d's, never being able to remember which is which. Difficulties such as these are repeated in spelling and in knowing how any group of words, letters or numbers is ordered. If problems of this sort are not recognized and allowance made for them, it won't be surprising if sufferers from them make others suffer in the classroom. Much of what will be going on in eleven year-olds' school work will depend on their ability to read and make sense of written material, and in turn to write for themselves. Children (and it is more often boys than girls) with this sort of problem may not be able to make much sense of some lessons.

Little wonder that they make trouble. However, specialized help can be found for such children once their problems have been diagnosed. Growing recognition of their difficulties among educationalists means that they may be allowed to use word processors (which they often find easier for writing) and allowed increased time for working in an examination setting.

Slow learners

This sort of specific learning difficulty, while not too common, is increasingly recognized and efforts are made to provide help. For yet other children, problems with their learning may need different sorts of solution, and may involve recognition of their more severe limitations, requiring more intensive help or a change of school. These are the children who have probably always been slow in understanding and learning.

Jon for example had always been slow. He had been slow to be born, slow to sit up, to walk and to talk. He had been slow at school too, but he was a likable, cheerful young boy and very popular with the other children. They were always happy if he tagged along with them and always willing to lend him a hand. His reading was hesitant, he stumbled over his times tables and his writing was laborious. Jon's parents had not really wanted to think about his difficulties, hoping he would grow out of them. However, the nature of the work he was required to do at his quite academic school changed when he was eleven. Jon became very anxious and depressed. Homework was a nightmare. Jon wanted to get on with it, but simply did not grasp what he had to do.

His parents had to help him but Jon became more upset each evening. His parents realized how hard he was trying and could see for themselves how difficult it was for him. They gradually came to face the fact that the school he was at and the work he had to do was too much for him. When they suggested he should go to a smaller school where children were supported in working at their own pace, Jon was both relieved and dismayed. He wanted to stay with his friends, but he knew the work was too much. He agreed to go to look at the smaller school, and having seen the sort of work that he would be doing, which looked much more like what he could do, he agreed to go. Jon still finds the work difficult, he always will, but the difficulty, once he had changed schools was not compounded by the anxious panic that he could not keep up with the others. Jon returned to his usual more serene self, able to develop his other abilities and no longer persecuted by his homework. He was still able to see friends from his old school as well as making new ones at his new school. His parents were glad, when they saw how he responded to the change, that they had faced up to their disappointment, recognized his weaknesses, and, in the process enabled him to make the best of his strengths.

The influence of feelings on school work

Perhaps the most common reason for children's failure in school work arises from problems in concentration. This happens when children are preoccupied with issues that have nothing to do with their work, but which are so pressing that they have little room for thinking about anything else. Problems of this kind have been mentioned already in other chapters. Jody, the girl who felt left at home while her family went out to work, and who watched TV and ate until they came home, was one such child. Her school performance was affected for a while by her feelings about her family. Andrea, the girl whose sexual maturity caused her to go out with girls older than herself for a while, also had little time for school work while she was preoccupied with her sexual status. Both these girls were helped back to an ordinary interest in their work by sensible action on the part of their parents and teachers.

All children go through periods of difficulty as they grow up, and eleven year-olds in particular may find their concentration difficult to maintain in the new academic situations in which they may find themselves. In particular, those children whose lives have been hard and who have experienced losses, neglect or abuse may find it difficult to allow their minds to move from the task of making sense of the stressful situations they have experienced, and to turn them to concepts such as mathematics, the political situation in British North America or to the imports and exports of Iceland. If a child is grappling with the loss of a mother or father (through death, divorce or for whatever reason) it is not surprising if he or she is unable to concentrate on what the teachers are saying.

Nor are the most disturbing preoccupations of eleven year-olds primarily contemporary ones. Problems like those of Jody and Andrea, which had to do with current troubles, are easier to deal with. By far the most complicated are those that the child has been grappling with for years, and has found ways of managing, but ways that may not be helpful now he or she is eleven. For example, many children have avoided thinking about painful feelings by being very active and practical and pushing their fears out of their minds. When they are eleven, more concentrated thinking is demanded of them in school and they may not be able to meet that demand without reviving thoughts and feelings that they have long dealt with by not thinking too much. This may pose a dilemma. Some children may respond by getting quite disturbingly preoccupied with the thoughts and feelings they have not wanted to face. Yet others may resort to their previous ways of coping, by pushing all serious thought away, and in doing so they may limit their capacity to tackle their school work.

Leila, for example, was very good at math and science, but could not cope with English and poetry, or any other subject that touched her feelings. She had to leave her native country suddenly a few years ago, leaving friends and family and beloved possessions, never to return. She had to be brave then, and she went on being brave, first of all not allowing her feelings to show and then later losing touch with any feelings that might actively have upset her. She was a very practical person who liked doing things and was good at doing. She could not think about anything that might remind her of how she had felt in the past and to do with what she had lost. She could use her ability in some respects, but not in others.

Leila's way of managing was to try to blot out certain feelings. Other children find other ways of trying to cope with difficult feelings. Some of these ways are equally unhelpful for an eleven year-old with a great deal to learn. Some may try to keep their minds off their troubles by doing things all the time, leaving no time for school work that requires them to think, as Leila did. Yet others might try to take their minds off their feelings by watching television day and night, absorbed in dramas on the screen instead of their own, thus allowing themselves no space for thoughts about school work.

Jason had found another way of coping with his life. He had been very close to his dad for the first few years of his life, but then his dad had returned to his own country, leaving Jason's mom with Jason and his two little sisters. Jason had not seen his dad since. At the time Jason was devastated. He was not very old and had decided, as many children of that age would, that his dad had left them because he, Jason, was such a bad boy. This was a very distressing idea and Jason had tried to make up for it by taking his father's place as the man of the house, looking after his mother and his sisters. Underneath he still felt as if he was bad, but by acting as the man of the house, he also felt quite important. He was the big one, he thought, and no one told him what to do.

In primary school he became very bossy, a leader, but also a child who thought he knew it all. He was a practical kid, and although he had some problems with reading, writing and arithmetic he managed all right, and if he did not understand something, he often got one of his gang to help him or do it for him. Teachers had found him quite a handful, but usually manageable. He enjoyed being one of the biggest in the school, organizing the younger ones as he did at home. All was reasonably well, until he changed schools when he was eleven. Then he wasn't the biggest one, and, worse than that, he was obliged to sit with all the others in his class listening and trying to understand what a lot of different teachers were saying to him. He had to read books and write essays. Jason felt little and inadequate and abandoned by a teacher at his other school of whom he had been fond—like his dad.

Jason became very difficult in school, talking and laughing in class, not turning up class, being rude and misbehaving. He was really expressing his feelings of being a bad boy whom his dad and his teacher had left. His teacher soon became very worried and his mother could no longer recognize her responsible son. She was very inclined to blame the school. Children like Jason frequently have trouble when the character of school and academic work changes. Whether such children can weather the changes will depend on how far the school and the family can work together to help these youngsters, and also the extent to which the child himself is able to acknowledge his need to be helped to adjust and to learn. Many parents are tempted to blame the school rather than seeing the problem as one that has to do with a total situation, including their own. If, however, co-operation is possible between all concerned, such a situation may be resolved without further professional help. Unless some action between the family and school at the earliest stage can be taken, that is to say when the child is eleven, he may get so set into disruptive ways that his future at school may be in jeopardy. Unless a child like Jason can find some way of managing school more adequately, he will fall further and further behind, thus making it more and more difficult for him to modify his disruptive behavior.

Not all parents find it easy to work with school and teachers in the interests of their children. Memories of their own schooldays, perhaps in former less-understanding times and places, may color their feelings about teachers and schools; going to talk about their child may feel to them like being sent to the principal's office again. However, it is important for you to be in good communication with your child's school. Parents need to know how their child is doing, where he or she needs help as well as when things are going well. Teachers need to know how the child is at home, and in particular, whether there are difficulties such as illness in the family with which the child has to struggle.

At no time is such co-operation more important than when your child is eleven. You need to know how your child is managing the changes and need to feel free to talk with teachers. If you are able to do so you will be able to give your child a good start academically. For parents who have had less satisfactory school experiences themselves, co-operation with the school will offer them the possibility of providing their children with a better start, and they might even be able to find a different perspective from which to re-evaluate their own experiences.

CHAPTER FIVE

FRIENDS AND INTERESTS

A theme that has run through the understanding of eleven-year-old children has been their drive towards greater independence. This is related to developing awareness of them selves, their increasing capacity to look after themselves, to think for themselves, and to know who they are and what they can do. Having mostly in the past been so dependent on parents, their growing capacities may cause them to begin to move away from their families, as has been said earlier, and to find things to do on their own or with friends.

Jean spends all her summer holidays in the stables. She had riding lessons when she was younger, but now that she is eleven her parents allow her to go off early in the morning (it isn't very far, just around the corner from where they live) and she is welcome at the stables where she helps groom the horses and muck them out. She helps with the younger children as well as having the opportunity to ride herself. Her parents do not see her for the rest of the day, though she could come home easily if anything went wrong. They are delighted that she has an interest and that she is learning how to look after the horses. Jean is totally absorbed in all these new skills and with the other people she meets there. Reasonably secure and sociable eleven year-olds do not feel they need their parents, but they *do* need others of their own age.

Groups and gangs

Children of eight, nine and ten tend to congregate in gangs of the same sex. A look in the school playground of an elementary school will reveal groups of girls together distinctly separated from groups of boys. By eleven these groups have usually become very stable, each child knowing what part they play within the group. Among the girls some may be growing up fast and beginning to move away, but most, girls and boys, will continue to be members of the groups that they have grown used to. Tony, for example, who was mentioned earlier, in his wish to go to a football game with his friends was well able to go to places and do things with his friends that he would have been scared of had he had to go on his own. The social life and the leisure interests of most children of this age are based on the familiar group, and the group is therefore of paramount importance to them.

Girls' groups

The girls' groups of contemporaries will be more likely to be beginning to break up than will the boys' groups. Girls of eleven are occasionally, like Andrea (described before), wanting to strike out on their own, either with older girls, or sometimes with older boys. Very often such children, like Andrea, after a period of experimentation return to more age-appropriate behavior. Parents may need to be sensitive and understanding, as Andrea's parents were, as well as firm, reminding their daughters how young and inexperienced they are, if they are not to be seen as either too old-fashioned—thus perpetuating rebellion—or as not concerned about their daughters' risky precocity.

Girls' groups, quite apart from their earlier maturation, are a bit different from boys'. Girls have a tendency to have a best friend, and the groups that come into being in elementary schools are often groups of best friends. These groups may experience a lot of best-friend swapping, which can be the cause of a lot of heartaches among members. It is very hard for parents to look on while children suffer, and it is often difficult not to intervene by talking to ex-friends' parents, or joining in with the daughter's denigration of an estranged friend. But, in some ways, these social dramas help the girl to sort out where she is in relation to other people. The ups and downs of social life enable her to observe the effect of her behavior on others, and theirs on her. Whereas a younger child might not be able to see relationships in this way, the eleven year-old can begin to do so, and the girl's social adventures within her group enable her to sort out who she is, how to behave and to think about the behavior of others as well.

Most children of this age behave badly to their friends sometimes, and as a parent you may feel outraged on behalf of your daughter. A calm opportunity to talk with your daughter about the difficulties she is experiencing, expressing care and concern for her but without taking sides, can enhance her understanding and can set her on her way towards more mature relationships.

Boys' groups and gangs

Groups of average eleven-year-old boys seem to get into mischief quite a bit, but often groups of boys of this age get together in pursuit of some interest. Groups of boys are on the whole less interested in their relationships with each other than in what they are doing. For doing something—playing football, skateboarding, making model aircraft, playing with remote-controlled cars—is likely to be what they are up to. Boys of this age are quite competitive, and they may well get upset with each other about winning or if one possesses something that another wants. There are plenty of reasons why boys may fall out with each other, and if they do they may well get physical, and fight it out. Many eleven year-olds, however, will be able to control their wish to fight and can turn their anger into words. Boys (and indeed girls) of eleven may well be in possession of a large range of swear words and be prepared to use them. Many parents do not regard swearing with much more favor than fighting, and it is true that a child's verbal abuse can seem very violent. On the other hand, saying something is better than actually hitting someone. Some parents might think that a verbal slinging match is preferable to fighting it out at this age. Such parents will be hoping that their eleven year-old will soon find ways of dealing with anger, other than by swearing, and that their son will in due course grow out of swearing. Children of parents who do not swear much usually follow their example by finding other ways of dealing with disturbing feelings.

Boys' groups evoke a great deal of loyalty amongst their members. Competition and rivalry may exist within them, though there are well established roles (for example, of leader), but the really strong rivalry usually exists between one group and another. Not only groups of boys, but also groups of girls, and indeed many groups, buy internal harmony at the price of having external enemies. This is appropriate at eleven years of age. In their future development many boys will find other ways of managing hostile feelings.

The groups in which boys and girls of eleven continue to exist are very important as places to practice relationships with others. These groups are likely to break up as adolescent pairings develop during the teenage years. For many children the carefree existence of the pre-adolescent years provides some of the most socially satisfying years of their lives. Many eleven year-olds make friends who will last for life.

Not being able to make friends

But what of children who find it difficult to make friends and who, therefore, are not members of groups or gangs? Parents of such children will have found, for the most part, that this is not a new problem. The eleven year-old who has difficulty making friends will previously have been the eight, nine and ten year-old with the same problem.

Parents will probably notice that such children are anxious about their relationships within the family as well, particularly with their mothers. Children who have felt secure and confident as babies with their mothers are usually the ones who are most popular and sought after as friends. Parents who are aware of problems underlying their children's difficulties may be able to help by taking into consideration what might have contributed to the difficulty in earlier years.

Rose was the only child of a single mother and, in some ways, they were very close. Life had been pretty difficult for Rose's mother when Rose was a baby, although she was a much wanted child. Her mother had been worried about her and how to look after her properly while maintaining her own studies. The babysitters she had found had not worked out very well and Rose's mother had been constantly distressed about the circumstances in which she was leaving her baby. Once her course of study was complete, Rose's mother relaxed and could spend more time with Rose, but Rose continued to be distressed whenever she was left, and to fret for her mother. Rose's first few days at kindergarten were a nightmare, but ultimately she found ways to manage herself, mostly by following the teacher around and trying to help. While the beginning of the school year could be difficult if Rose had to get used to a new teacher, on the whole she managed and quite enjoyed her early schooling. She occasionally visited the homes of some of the other little girls, but something usually seemed to go wrong in the end and Rose would have to come home to her mother.

When Rose was nearly eleven, Rose's mother was anxious that Rose should settle easily into sixth grade because up until now she had been working part-time to be available for her daughter, but she was planning, now that Rose was older, to take on more work. Rose's mother went to talk to her teacher. Rose's grade five teacher was also concerned about Rose , and to hear that Rose's mother was thinking of making a career move. She talked about her concern that leaving Rose to her own devices a bit more at this time might really upset her. Her mother resolved to talk with Rose and make it clear that she would be there for her after school as usual, having decided, for the moment, not to take on more work. Her fifth grade teacher consulted the principal about Rose's problem, so that she would be careful about the class into which she would be placed. In fact, in her new class was a girl who had newly moved to the neighborhood and who did not have many friends or acquaintances and Rose shyly got to know this new girl. It took a long time before Rose settled down, and she really clung to her new friend for years, but her mother's awareness and preparedness to take account of the nature of Rose's difficulties, enabled Rose to be more confident and to make a hesitant new start.

Rose was perhaps fortunate. Other children whose problems arise from ongoing, unhappy family relationships may find ways of avoiding all relationships with their contemporaries. Jason, mentioned earlier in relation to the trouble that he experienced when changing schools, thought he had friends, but really they were partners in rebellion and he was constantly upset when they let him down. His only way of being with other children was to be the boss and this did not win him friends.

Yet other children find activities which isolate them. Many children of this age who have trouble keeping friends, also have trouble in finding things to do that interest them. It is noticeable that the most popular eleven year-olds are often those who have ideas about what to do. These ideas carry the others with them. Lonely children often take refuge in the television. Such children find it more satisfactory to have relationships by proxy with those on the screen. Absorbed in their imaginary lives, isolated children do not have to give and take with real friends. In their imaginations, lonely children can also be in control of the situation.

Computers, as well as the television, often offer solace to the child without friends. Playing computer or video games invariably involves being in control. The fear of loss of control often lies behind a child's difficulty with other children. Computer games are all-absorbing and transport the child away from the sorrows and frustrations of ordinary life, into a world where they call the tune. Computer games can become very addictive, pulling children away from the real world and from real people. Many eleven year-olds go through a phase of absorption in computer or video games. Most pull out of it, either joining forces with other children in their pursuit or moving on to more mature interests in using computers, or simply by getting bored. Some, who really fear being with other children, may continue to be absorbed with such games and so go on dodging the difficult ups and downs of relationships with others. At eleven, parents of children absorbed in computers probably do not need to worry too much. If this absorption continues, to the exclusion of other interests, parents may then feel the need to take thought, and possibly seek professional advice.

Bullying and aggression

Some children who avoid others may complain of bullying, and base their avoidance of other children on their conviction that other children will be mean to them. Some children may have had experiences at school on which this conviction is well founded. Others who complain of being bullied have in the past done some bullying themselves. Philip, aged eleven, complained of being bullied at his school. His mother was surprised, since in the past it had been he who had been accused of being cruel to younger children. His parents were in the process of a divorce, his mother being unable to tolerate her husband's violence any longer. Philip was fond of his dad and did not want his parents to split up. But his mother was convinced that his father had often been jealous of their son and had been rough and unkind to him. She knew that, in the past, when he had been upset Philip had taken it out on other children. Now that he felt his father was suffering, he felt guilty and got himself abused.

It is rare for children who have not been bullied or abused themselves to abuse others. Parents who can control themselves show, by their example, how children should manage their own upset and angry feelings by not passing them on to others. Parents who can reflect calmly on their anger are likely, in turn, to have calm and thoughtful children. To think anger through is not likely to be a comfortable process, for it may mean accepting some responsibility for difficulties, but in the long run life can be made easier for parent and child alike if difficulties can be thought about and talked over. And it is much easier to talk things over now the child is eleven years old.

Marek's father was really cross with him because Marek had not told him about the parents' night at school and he had arranged an important business meeting for the same evening. He wanted to meet Marek's teachers very much. He wondered if Marek had deliberately not told him until after he had arranged this meeting because he did not want him to go to the parents' night. What could it be that he did not want his father to know? Marek's father became suspicious and angry. He would really tell Marek off when he got home. Then he began to think. When had he last seen Marek? He had been working late for the last few evenings and had hardly seen his son. As he thought, he got a bit less angry. Perhaps his meeting could be postponed. Coming home early, he managed not to raise the matter at once. He overheard Marek grumbling to his mother about a hurried homework assignment, due to a serious defect in the school's main photocopier. When he spoke to Marek, he was still very indignant about the short notice of the parents' night they had been given. Marek said he had been asked to apologize for the short notice, and to explain about the photocopier. He had told his mom, but had not been able to tell his dad because he had not seen him. His mom had forgotten to let his dad know about the photocopier because when she had told him about the meeting, he had been so cross. Marek's dad was glad he had not been cross with Marek for something that was not really his fault. He went to the parents night briefly, before his other appointment, and heard that his son was doing very well. He was pleased he had made the effort, for, when he had been so angry he had thought of punishing Marek by not attending. In the long run, and if he had continued to be suspicious of Marek, things might not have been so happy for Marek at school. Marek learned that his father did not always act immediately when he was cross, but that stopping to think is helpful in the long run.

This goes not just for uncomfortably angry feelings but for others as well. Parents who can talk about what they feel with their children can share good things as well as bad. However parents who control their feelings tightly with a stiff upper lip, or who cannot bear their children to express their emotions, convey to their children that they should not show their feelings. Children who bottle up their feelings may not be able to keep the cork in all the time! Such children may erupt into extremes of feeling of all kinds, weeping uncontrollably or lashing out.

The combination of parental violence and disapproval of any show of emotion, may put children in an intolerable position—indignant at how they are treated, yet with no means of communicating their distress. In such positions it is not surprising if children explode into violence and even criminal violence. If no one ever seems to have taken account of their feelings, they may conclude that they have no need to take account of those of anyone else.

Of course some children may not be able to appreciate the extent to which their feelings are recognized and understood by the grown-ups. Some children may not feel understood unless the adult does exactly what they want. There are, however, a small number of children whose experience of life has not enabled them to know that anyone cares about them or what they feel. Such children are in danger of acting their feelings out without any concern for others.

Parents are crucial in shaping the behavior of their children. Teachers and circumstances may modify or exacerbate what children do but for most eleven year-olds their parents' example is often enough to help them manage their feelings. Most eleven year-olds will not bully and generally will have enough self-confidence not to allow themselves to be bullied. All eleven year-olds will sometimes feel furious. How they express this fury—by hitting out, by swearing, by crying, by passing it on by bullying, by sulking, pretending it didn't happen or by talking it over, depends on the responses of those around to the child over the years. Eleven could be an age at which children's responses mature and become more thoughtful along with the rest of their development. If you are able to accept your children's anger and talk with them about it, your children can be helped to think and talk before acting destructively.

Competition and co-operation

The growing self-awareness of eleven year-olds, taken together with the increasing emphasis on educational performance and competitive games, tends to make them look at each other and compare. Painful rivalries may develop. Some of the rivalry may be taken up with one group against another. Parents can also be helpful in taking the edge from inevitable disappointments and failures, when children look at their companions and find that their own performance is not as good in some respects. Competition can sometimes be a spur to greater effort, but for many children it is as likely to provoke despair and a tendency to give up. Even children who seem to be doing well can be dismayed if parents urge them to maintain their position at the top of the class. Those who have tried very hard and only achieved mediocre results can be thoroughly disheartened if urged to greater efforts. One man remembered with passion his hatred of a boy with whom he vied for tenth or eleventh place in class throughout his schooldays. In adult life he is quite a successful man but permanently haunted by a terror of failure that undermines the quality of his life. You can help your children with these uncomfortable comparisons if you are not too concerned about how your child is doing in relation to the rest of the class. Parents who are more concerned that their child is doing his or her best, than where this places them in relation to others, will be the most likely to support their child's work. Such an attitude conveys to the child the fundamental interest of the parent in the child him or herself, not in the child's capacity to be better than some other child. Children supported by such parents will be able to work for themselves and thus do as well as they can. This will also enhance their developing sense of themselves.

In savoring their developing independence and feeling of individuality, many eleven year-olds are also more able to observe and think about others. Such children are much more tolerant of shortcomings than they have been previously, and seeing friends in need of help, can offer a hand, with more understanding than they have when younger. Children of any age can be kind and sympathetic to one another, but at eleven helpfulness can be based on some understanding of the predicament of the other person. Sharon, for example, who was the friend that Rose made in her sixth grade class, was very tolerant of Rose's occasional panics about her mother, and her tantrums if she got really unsure about where her mother was. Sharon knew her friend and knew she would get over it. She knew that she herself was lucky enough to have a large family, where there would always be someone around to give her a hand, and could appreciate Rose's fear of being without anyone to rely on.

One of the factors affecting the growing understanding of others is the increasing capacity of the eleven year-old to put thoughts and feelings into words. A younger Sharon confronted by an awkward Rose might have simply walked away from her or had a fight. The eleven-year-old Sharon could ask Rose what the trouble was. Rose was not always able to tell her clearly, but then they would try to sort it out between them, and begin to appreciate what each other felt. Although eleven year-olds enjoy doing things together, they also have more capacity to exchange ideas with each other than they had before.

Within social structures familiar to them from younger days, eleven year-olds try out the social skills of observation and conversation that they will need more and more during their adolescence and in later life.

Conclusion

Tim, the first eleven year-old mentioned in this book, was puzzled about entering his twelfth year. His parents were too, feeling that eleven is an "in-between time." They are right. But in-between times are important and busy times, as we have seen. Tim had a lot of thinking to do during that year. And so did his parents. Tim needed to move gradually away from his earlier childhood preoccupations and to prepare for a more responsible, and in some ways, more self-aware way of life. He had to bid farewell to some of his more impulsive carefree behavior and become more thoughtful. This is not just something that was demanded at school, and he seemed able to cope with school anyway, but it influenced everything—his relationships at home and at school and his life with friends outside school. It even affected his physical growth, to the extent that in filling out, he began to think of further growth to come.

As we have seen, all these developments, while exciting, can also seem daunting. Eleven year-olds experiment and often make mistakes. We all do all the time, but people at the beginning of things often make more then than at other times, and eleven year-olds are on the brink of major change. Eleven year-olds therefore really need understanding parents who will recognize their uncertain moves towards growth, and their retreats into more childlike behavior. Eleven year-olds are beginning to be able to talk about themselves and what is happening to them. Most will not have reached the full crisis of adolescent rebellion. Many parents, therefore, with any luck will be able to talk with their eleven year-olds and to give them a hand in thinking about what is happening to them. Their help, if tactfully offered within the context of an ongoing good-enough relationship, will probably be appreciated by their children and valuable to them in finding their way ahead.

It is important for you and your eleven year-old to think about and face up to the changes that are around. Changes imply adaptations in behavior and both parents and children have to fit in with the demands of your child's growth. Families that can talk about it will find these changes the least disconcerting.

Eleven can be an interesting age if thoughtfully approached by parents and children. Adaptation to changes at this age can lay the foundation for a relatively smooth transition to adolescence.

FURTHER READING

What's Happening to My Body?, Lynda Madaras, Penguin,1989
Narratives of Love and Loss, Margaret and Michael Rustin, Verso, 1989
The Emotional Experience of Learning and Teaching, Isca Salzberger-
Wittenberg, Gianna Henry & Elsie Osborne, Routledge & Kegan
Paul, London, 1983
Parenting Threads, Caring for Children When Couples Part, National
Stepfamily Association, 1992

The Author

Eileen Orford is a Consultant Child Psychotherapist working in the Child and Family Department of the Tavistock Clinic. She is also Vice-Chair of the Clinic. Before becoming a Child Psychotherapist, she lectured in psychology and worked in vocational guidance. As well as working directly with children, she also consults to organizations and professionals working with children, and spent some years working with tutors to the First Year of a Comprehensive School, and therefore thinking about eleven year-olds. Eileen Orford is married with a grown up son.

UNDERSTANDING YOUR CHILD
TITLES IN THIS SERIES

Price per volume: $8.95 + $2.00 for shipping and handling

Please send your name, address and total amount to:

WARWICK PUBLISHING INC.
388 KING STREET WEST • SUITE 111
TORONTO, ONTARIO M5V 1K2